BEAT THE WHEAT!

Easy and Delicious Wheat-Free Recipes for Kids With Allergies

by KATRINA JORGENSEN

CONSULTANT
Amy Durkan MS, RDN, CDN
Nutrition Research Manager
Mount Sinai Medical Center
New York, NY

CAPSTONE PRESS
a capstone imprint

Edge Books are published by Capstone Press,
1710 Roe Crest Drive, North Mankato, Minnesota 56003
www.mycapstone.com

Library of Congress Cataloging-in-Publication Data
Cataloging-in-Publication data is on file with the Library of Congress.
ISBN 978-1-4914-8057-1 (library binding)
ISBN 978-1-4914-8062-5 (eBook PDF)

Editorial Credits
Anna Butzer, editor; Heidi Thompson, designer; Morgan Walters, media researcher;
Sarah Schuette, food stylist; Kathy McColley, production specialist

Design Elements
Shutterstock: avian, design element, Katerina Kirilova, design element, Lena Pan, design
element, Marco Govel, design element, mexrix, design element, Sabina Pittak, design
element, STILLFX, design element, swatchandsoda, design element

Photography by Capstone Studio: Karon Dubke

Editor's note:
Capstone cannot ensure that any food is allergen-free. The only way to be sure a food is
safe is to read all labels carefully, every time. Cross-contamination is also a risk for those
with food allergies. Please call food companies to make sure their manufacturing processes
avoid cross-contamination. Also, always be sure to clean hands, surfaces, and tools
before cooking.

Printed and bound in the USA.
009675F16

TABLE OF CONTENTS

WHAT IS A FOOD ALLERGY?

Our bodies are armed with immune systems. It's the immune system's job to fight infections, viruses, and invaders. Sometimes the immune system identifies a certain food as one of these invaders and attacks it. While our immune system fights, a chemical response is triggered and causes an allergic reaction. Reactions vary greatly from a mild skin irritation to having trouble breathing. Any time you feel you are having a reaction, tell an adult immediately.

The best way to avoid having an allergic reaction is to be aware of what you are eating. Be careful not to consume that allergen. If you are not sure if that allergen is in a food, ask an adult or read the ingredient label of the food container before eating. Unfortunately, allergens can sometimes be hard to identify in an ingredient list. Check out http://www.foodallergy.org for a full list of hidden wheat terms.

Avoiding food allergens can be hard to manage, especially when they are found in so many of our favorite foods. This cookbook will take you on a culinary journey to explore many of the dishes you've had to avoid because of a wheat allergy.

Kitchen Safety

A safe kitchen is a fun kitchen! Always start your recipes with clean hands, surfaces, and tools. Wash your hands and any tools you may use in future steps of a recipe, especially when handling raw meat. Make sure you have an adult nearby to help you with any task you don't feel comfortable doing, such as cutting vegetables or carrying hot pans.

Have other food allergies? No problem.
Check out the list at the end of each recipe
for substitutions for other common allergens.
Look out for other cool tips and ideas too!

CONVERSIONS

1/4 teaspoon	1.25 grams or milliliters
1/2 teaspoon	2.5 g or mL
1 teaspoon	5 g or mL
1 tablespoon	15 g or mL
1/4 cup	57 g (dry) or 60 mL (liquid)
1/3 cup	75 g (dry) or 80 mL (liquid)
1/2 cup	114 g (dry) or 125 mL (liquid)
2/3 cup	150 g (dry) or 160 mL (liquid)
3/4 cup	170 g (dry) or 175 mL (liquid)
1 cup	227 g (dry) or 240 mL (liquid)
1 quart	950 mL

Fahrenheit (°F)	Celsius (°C)
325°	160°
350°	180°
375°	190°
400°	200°
425°	220°
450°	230°

FLUFFY

Looking for a hearty breakfast that's quick, easy, and wheat-free? These pancakes stack up to their name—light, airy, and delicious! Ditch the wheat with this breakfast delight, and don't forget the maple syrup!

Prep Time: 5 minutes

Cook Time: 10 minutes

Serves 4

Ingredients

1 cup wheat-free flour blend

2 teaspoons baking powder

2 tablespoons sugar

pinch of salt

1 cup buttermilk

1 egg

2 tablespoons oil

1 teaspoon vanilla extract

cooking spray

maple syrup, for serving

Tools

measuring cups/spoons

large mixing bowl

electric hand mixer with whisk
attachment

non-stick skillet

spatula

plate

Allergen Alert!

If you're avoiding dairy, you can make your
own dairy-free buttermilk! Simply mix
1 tablespoon lemon juice with 1 cup
dairy-free milk such as almond or rice milk.
Allow mixture to sit for five minutes and
then stir before adding to the recipe!

No eggs? No problem. Instead of
an egg, use one mashed-up banana.

1. Combine the flour, baking powder, sugar, salt, buttermilk, egg, oil, and vanilla extract in a large bowl.

2. Mix the ingredients until mostly smooth using an electric hand mixer set on medium.

3. Place the non-stick skillet on a burner set on medium heat and spray lightly with cooking spray.

4. Spoon about 1/3 of a cup onto the hot pan.

5. Flip the pancake over when bubbles start to form around the edges of the pancake.

6. Continue cooking an additional two minutes or until golden brown on both sides.

7. Place cooked pancake on a plate and set aside.

8. Repeat steps 4 through 6 until all batter is used up.

9. Serve hot with maple syrup.

PUMPKIN MORNING **MUFFINS**

Pumpkins may be a staple of Halloween, but with this recipe, you can enjoy them year-round! This festive fall sweet treat is packed with Vitamin A, an essential nutrient that keeps your vision sharp.

Prep Time: 15 minutes

Cook Time: 30 minutes

Makes 12 muffins

Ingredients

1 tart apple, such as Granny Smith

2 carrots

⅓ cup oil

1 15-ounce can pumpkin puree

¼ cup sugar

¼ cup brown sugar

1 teaspoon maple extract

2 cups wheat-free flour blend

2 teaspoons baking soda

1 teaspoon ground cinnamon

½ teaspoon ground ginger

¼ teaspoon ground cloves

¼ teaspoon salt

½ cup raisins

Tools

standard muffin tin with 12 cups

paper muffin liners

cutting board

vegetable peeler

chef's knife

spoon

box grater

large mixing bowl

measuring cups/spoons

1. Preheat oven to 350°F. Place one liner in each of the cups of the muffin tin and set aside.

2. Peel the apple with the vegetable peeler. Then cut out the core by cutting the apple in half from top to bottom. Chop the apple into small cubes and set aside.

3. Peel the carrots with the vegetable peeler. Grate the carrots using the large-holed side of a box grater. Set aside.

4. In a large mixing bowl, combine the oil, pumpkin, sugar, brown sugar, and maple extract. Stir to combine.

5. Add the flour, baking soda, cinnamon, ginger, cloves, and salt. Stir until all the flour is absorbed. It's OK if the mix is a little lumpy.

6. Add the apples, carrots, and raisins to the bowl and mix.

7. Scoop the batter evenly into the muffin tin, filling each muffin about two-thirds full.

8. Bake for 30–35 minutes, or until a toothpick inserted into the center of a muffin comes out clean.

CHEF'S TIP

Freeze leftover muffins and grab one in the morning for a quick on-the-go breakfast!

Allergens Eradicated!

No major food allergens found here!

MAPLE SAUSAGE BITES

Good (and delicious) things come in small packages! Store-bought sausages often use wheat as a filler, but these homemade bites are wheat-free. Spicy and sweet flavors combine in these tiny breakfast sausages.

Prep Time: 15 minutes

Cook Time: 10 minutes

Serves 4

Ingredients

1 pound (16 ounces) ground pork or turkey

½ teaspoon dried sage

½ teaspoon Italian seasoning

¼ teaspoon allspice

½ teaspoon seasoning salt

¼ teaspoon ground black pepper

1 teaspoon fennel seeds

1 teaspoon pure maple syrup

Tools

mixing bowl

measuring spoons

fork

non-stick skillet

spatula

Allergens Eradicated!

No major food allergens found here!

1. Combine the ground pork or turkey, dried sage, Italian seasoning, allspice, seasoning salt, black pepper, fennel seeds, and maple syrup in a mixing bowl.

2. Mix with a fork until well-blended.

3. Split the mixture into 12 equal pieces and form into small, flat, round patties.

4. Place a non-stick skillet on a burner set to medium heat.

5. Add 3 or 4 patties to the pan and cook until browned on one side, two to three minutes.

6. Using the spatula, flip the patties. Cook an additional two to three minutes, or until no longer pink inside.

7. Repeat steps 5 and 6 until all the patties are cooked.

8. Serve hot as a side to your favorite breakfast!

CHEF'S TIP

If you are worried your hands will get too sticky handling the sausage mixture, rub a little oil on your palms beforehand!

RAISIN GRANOLA

It's important to eat breakfast before you start your day, but that can be tough when so many breakfast foods—especially cereal—contain wheat. With this recipe, you not only get a healthy substitute for cereal, you can take the leftovers with you for an on-the-go snack!

Prep Time: 10 minutes

Cook Time: 20 minutes

Serves 4

Ingredients

2 cups wheat-free rolled oats

½ cup wheat-free rice cereal

1 teaspoon ground cinnamon

¼ teaspoon salt

2 tablespoons brown sugar

⅓ cup pure maple syrup

⅓ cup oil, such as light olive oil

½ teaspoon vanilla

1 cup raisins

Tools

large baking sheet

parchment paper

mixing bowl

measuring cups/spoons

spatula

1. Preheat oven to 325°F. Place a sheet of parchment paper on a large baking sheet and set aside.

2. Combine the rolled oats, rice cereal, ground cinnamon, salt, brown sugar, maple syrup, oil, vanilla, and raisins in a mixing bowl. Stir until the ingredients are coated well.

3. Spread the granola mixture on the baking sheet so it is mostly flat.

4. Bake in the oven for 20 minutes or until slightly golden brown.

5. Remove from the oven and allow to cool before serving.

6. Eat with your favorite yogurt, or splash some milk on top for a crunchy breakfast treat!

7. Store leftovers in an airtight container for up to two weeks.

Allergens Eradicated!

No major food allergens found here!

CHEF'S TIP

Do raisins wrinkle your nose? Add any of your favorite dried fruits to this granola instead, such as blueberries, cherries, apricots, or bananas!

CREAMY
MAC and CHEESE

Does your mouth water at the thought of ooey, gooey cheese? If so, then this recipe is for you! Satisfy your comfort food craving with a bowl of this delicious pasta dish that is rich in calcium.

Prep Time: 15 minutes

Cook Time: 15 minutes

Serves 4

Ingredients

8 ounces sharp cheddar cheese

2 quarts water

2 teaspoons salt

2 cups dry wheat-free pasta, such as rice pasta

2 tablespoons butter

2 tablespoons rice flour

2 cups milk

¼ teaspoon ground mustard

¼ teaspoon paprika

Tools

box grater

cutting board

large pot

measuring cups/spoons

medium saucepan

whisk

colander

spoon

Allergen Alert!

Cheese, butter, and milk a no-go? You can still achieve cheesy greatness by using your favorite dairy-free cheese, butter, and milk replacements.

1. Grate the cheese with a large-holed grater set on top of a cutting board. Set aside.

2. In the large pot, add the water and salt. Place on a burner set on high heat until the water begins to boil.

3. Add the wheat-free pasta. Reduce the heat to medium-high. Cook according to package directions until just tender.

4. Make cheese sauce while the pasta cooks. In the saucepan, melt butter over medium heat.

5. Add the rice flour and whisk until absorbed. The mixture should look like wet sand.

6. Slowly pour the milk in while whisking to avoid lumps. Bring the mixture to a gentle simmer. Keep whisking until it begins to thicken, about five minutes.

7. Stir in the cheese, ground mustard, and paprika until melted. If the sauce is too thick, add a little milk.

8. When the pasta is done, drain it in a colander and place back into the pot.

9. Pour the cheese sauce over the pasta and stir until coated with the sauce.

10. Serve hot in bowls.

CHEF'S TIP

Add your favorite vegetables or toppings such as broccoli, carrots, asparagus, tomatoes, bacon, chicken, or beef!

TACO LETTUCE CUPS

Some taco shells contain wheat, but that doesn't mean you have to take tacos off the menu! Using Boston lettuce leaves as the shells, you can whip up some tasty tacos in no time! Top these leafy "shells" with your favorite veggies and taco toppings!

Prep Time: 20 minutes

Cook Time: 15 minutes

Serves 4

Ingredients

1 pound (16 oz) lean ground beef or turkey

1 tablespoon chili powder

1 teaspoon ground cumin

½ teaspoon ground oregano

½ teaspoon paprika

½ teaspoon black pepper

¼ teaspoon onion powder

¼ teaspoon garlic powder

1 teaspoon salt

1 head Boston lettuce

Taco Fixings

corn

beans

tomatoes

avocados

onion

your favorite cheese

salsa

Tools

skillet

spoon

measuring spoons

clean kitchen towel

cutting board

chef's knife

serving bowls

1. In a skillet, brown the ground beef or turkey over medium heat, breaking up the meat into small pieces with a spoon.

2. Add the chili powder, cumin, oregano, paprika, black pepper, onion powder, garlic powder, and salt. Stir to combine and reduce heat to low.

3. Carefully remove the outer leaves from the head of lettuce and dispose of them. Pull off 12 leaves and wash them gently under cool running water. Pat them dry with the clean kitchen towel and set aside.

4. Prepare your taco fixings by chopping tomatoes into small pieces, dicing the avocado, cutting the onion, and grating the cheese. Place in bowls for serving.

5. Transfer the meat to a serving bowl and scoop about 2 tablespoons of meat into each lettuce cup. Then add fixings to your liking.

6. Wrap up tightly and enjoy.

CHEF'S TIP

Vegetarians, don't fret! You can skip the meat and use one can of drained black beans instead. You can also use 2 cups of chopped eggplant or butternut squash in step 1.

Allergens Eradicated!

No major food allergens found here!

CHICKEN ZOODLE SOUP

When you're feeling under the weather, nothing beats a piping hot bowl of chicken noodle soup. However, most types of pasta are made with wheat. To avoid wheat, make the change from noodle to zucchini zoodle!

Prep Time: 20 minutes

Cook Time: 1 ½ hours

Serves 4

Ingredients

1 pound (16 oz) chicken leg quarters

2 quarts water

2 carrots

2 stalks celery

1 small onion

1 tablespoon dried parsley

2 teaspoons salt

1 teaspoon black pepper

1 teaspoon garlic powder

1 teaspoon ground turmeric

½ teaspoon dried thyme

½ teaspoon dried oregano

1 large zucchini

Tools

large stockpot

measuring cups/spoons

vegetable peeler

cutting board

chef's knife

tongs

box grater

2 forks

Allergens Eradicated!

No major food allergens found here!

1. Place the chicken and water in a large stockpot. Set the pot on a burner set to medium-high heat until it begins to simmer. Reduce heat to medium and cook for about one hour until the meat is cooked.

2. Prepare the vegetables while the meat cooks. Peel the carrots with a vegetable peeler. Chop the carrots and celery into 1/4-inch (0.6-centimeter) rounds. Cut the onion in half, peel, and then chop into small pieces. Set aside.

3. After the meat is cooked, carefully remove it from the pot using tongs. Place on a cutting board to cool.

4. Add the carrots, celery, onion, dried parsley, salt, pepper, garlic powder, turmeric, thyme, and oregano to the liquid and stir. Increase heat to bring to a low boil. Then reduce heat to medium and cook for about 30 minutes.

5. While the vegetables cook, grate the zucchini with the large-holed side of a box grater. Set aside.

6. Carefully pull the meat off of the bones (use two forks to avoid burning your fingers). Set aside.

7. Add both the zucchini and chicken back to the liquid. Stir for about one minute until the zucchini is cooked.

8. Serve hot in bowls with wheat-free crackers, if desired.

CHEF'S TIP

Craving carbs? Add 1 cup of rice to the pot during step 4.

CHICKEN PARMESAN
STUFFED PEPPERS

What do you get when you cross chicken Parmesan and stuffed peppers? Two mouthwatering entrees rolled into one! Wheat-free bread crumbs top off this recipe to give it a delightful crunch.

Prep Time: 20 minutes

Cook Time: 30 minutes

Serves 4

Ingredients

1 pound (16 oz) chicken breasts

½ teaspoon salt

¼ teaspoon pepper

3 teaspoons olive oil

4 bell peppers

1 cup marinara sauce

4 slices mozzarella cheese

½ cup Parmesan cheese

½ cup wheat-free bread crumbs

Tools

cutting board

chef's knife

measuring cups/spoons

skillet

small mixing bowl

spoon

8 x 8-inch (20 x 20-cm) baking dish

Allergen Alert!

You can still go Italian without
all the cheese. Skip the mozzarella
and replace the Parmesan with
¼ cup nutritional yeast for
a cheesy flavor without the dairy!

1. Preheat oven to 350°F.

2. Cut the chicken breasts in 1-inch (2.5-cm) cubes. Sprinkle salt and pepper on the cubes and set aside.

3. Place 2 teaspoons olive oil in a skillet and place on a burner set to medium heat.

4. Add the chicken and cook until no longer pink inside, about five to six minutes.

5. While the chicken cooks, cut off the tops of the bell peppers and scoop out the seeds and white ribs inside.

6. Pour the marinara sauce in with the chicken and stir until coated.

7. Place 1 slice of mozzarella cheese in the bottom of each pepper.

8. Evenly scoop the chicken into each pepper.

9. In a small bowl, combine the Parmesan cheese, bread crumbs, and 1 teaspoon olive oil and stir.

10. Sprinkle the bread crumb mixture evenly over the top of each pepper.

11. Place the peppers in the baking dish. Bake for about 30 minutes or until the peppers are slightly tender and topping is golden brown.

12. Serve hot.

SWEET POTATO
SHEPHERD'S PIE

Warm and comforting, this dish is
sure to satisfy your hunger. As an
added bonus, it is also rich in vitamins
and protein. Have fun serving up a
sweetened, wheat-free spin on this
English classic.

Prep Time: 15 minutes

Cook Time: 1 hour

Serves 4

Ingredients

4 medium sweet potatoes

2 quarts water

1 small onion

1 teaspoon olive oil

1 pound (16 oz) lean ground beef or turkey

1 cup beef broth

1 teaspoon coconut aminos

1 tablespoon tomato paste

1 teaspoon garlic powder

4 tablespoons butter

1 teaspoon salt

½ teaspoon ground black pepper

¼ teaspoon paprika

1 cup frozen vegetable mix (carrots, corn, peas)

Tools

vegetable peeler

chef's knife

cutting board

measuring cups/spoons

medium pot

large skillet

spoon

colander

potato masher

8 x 8-inch (20 x 20-cm) baking dish

spatula

1. Preheat oven to 325°F.

2. Peel and chop the potatoes. Place them in the pot and fill with water. Place on a burner set to high heat and boil. Reduce heat to medium and cook for 15 minutes or until tender.

3. Peel and chop the onion. Set aside.

4. Place skillet on a burner and set to medium heat. Add oil and onions. Cook for two minutes, stirring gently.

5. Place meat in skillet and break up into small pieces with a spoon. Cook until no longer pink, about eight minutes.

6. Add the broth, aminos, tomato paste, and garlic powder to the skillet. Stir to combine. Reduce heat to low and allow to simmer gently.

7. Drain the potatoes, return to pot, and mash. Add butter, salt, pepper, and paprika. Mash until smooth.

8. Add frozen vegetables to the skillet. Stir to combine.

9. Pour the meat mixture into the baking dish. Spread potatoes on top with a spatula.

10. Bake for 40 minutes, or until the top of the sweet potatoes is slightly browned.

11. Allow to cool for five minutes before serving hot in bowls.

CHEF'S TIP

Not sweet on sweet potatoes? You can use regular white potatoes in this recipe instead.

BAKED **FRENCH FRIES**

High in Vitamin C and potassium, potatoes are a great addition to your daily intake. Baking these delicious French fries is more heart-healthy too! Grab some spuds and create your own homemade fries with this quick and simple recipe.

Prep Time: 15 minutes

Cook Time: 30 minutes

Serves 4

Ingredients

4 medium potatoes

2 tablespoons oil, such as olive oil

½ teaspoon salt

¼ teaspoon pepper

Tools

large baking sheet

parchment paper

vegetable peeler

cutting board

chef's knife

paper towels

measuring spoons

mixing bowl

spatula

Allergens Eradicated!

No major food allergens found here!

1. Preheat oven to 425°F. Line the baking sheet with parchment paper. Set aside.

2. Peel the potatoes. Carefully cut each potato into three pieces lengthwise. Then cut each section into 4 or 5 pieces lengthwise, making long sticks.

3. Rinse the potato sticks and dry well with paper towels.

4. Place the sticks in the mixing bowl with the oil, salt, and pepper. Toss gently to coat evenly.

5. Spread the sticks on the baking sheet, making sure they are not stacked on top of each other.

6. Bake for about 15 minutes. Using a spatula, carefully flip over the fries. Bake an additional 15 minutes or until deep golden brown and crispy.

7. Remove from oven and allow to cool for five minutes before serving.

CHEF'S TIP

Get fancy with your fries
and add some fun flavors:
Italian Fries: Add 1 teaspoon
Italian seasoning during step 4.
Spicy Buffalo Fries: Add ¼ teaspoon
cayenne pepper during step 4.

BLTA PASTA SALAD

You don't need to make a sandwich to enjoy the classic flavors of a BLT. Bacon, lettuce, tomato, avocado, and pasta are the perfect players for a refreshing, scrumptious salad.

Prep Time: 3 hours 20 minutes
(3 hours inactive)

Cook Time: 45 minutes

Serves 4

Ingredients

2 quarts water

2 teaspoons salt

1 cup wheat-free pasta

2 tablespoons Dijon mustard

2 tablespoons apple cider vinegar

¼ cup extra-virgin olive oil

2 teaspoons honey

3 slices wheat-free bacon

2 tomatoes

1 head romaine lettuce

1 avocado

Tools

medium pot

measuring cups/spoons

colander

medium bowl

small mixing bowl

whisk

skillet

cutting board

chef's knife

large mixing bowl

tongs

Allergens Eradicated!

No major food allergens found here!

1. Add water and salt to a pot and place on a burner set to high heat to boil. Add the pasta and cook according to package directions.

2. Drain the pasta and rinse with cool water.

3. Place pasta in a medium bowl. Cover and place in a refrigerator for at least three hours to cool completely.

4. While the pasta cools, make the dressing. In a small mixing bowl, combine the Dijon mustard, vinegar, olive oil, and honey. Whisk quickly until it is smooth and no longer separated. Add salt if needed.

5. Cook the bacon in a skillet until crisp. Chop the bacon on a cutting board. Set aside.

6. Chop the tomato and lettuce. Set aside.

7. With an adult's help, cut the avocado open and remove the pit. Scoop out the pulp and chop it. Set aside.

8. To assemble, put the cooled pasta, dressing, bacon, tomato, lettuce, and avocado in a large mixing bowl. Toss gently with tongs.

9. Allow to rest about 15 minutes before serving. Store leftovers in a refrigerator for up to five days.

APPLE CAKE

Apple pie is a classic American dessert, but have you ever tried apple cake? Besides being delicious, apples are also high in Vitamin C and fiber. Enjoy making this cake studded with pieces of autumn's favorite fruit!

Prep Time: 20 minutes

Cook Time: 45 minutes

Serves 6

Ingredients

cooking spray

2 cups wheat-free flour blend

1 teaspoon cinnamon

1 teaspoon baking soda

1 teaspoon baking powder

¼ teaspoon salt

1 ½ cups sugar

¾ cup light olive oil

1 teaspoon vanilla extract

3 eggs

3 tart apples

Tools

8 x 8-inch (20 x 20-cm) baking dish

2 medium mixing bowls

measuring cups/spoons

electric mixer

vegetable peeler

cutting board

chef's knife

toothpick

Allergen Alert!

If you need to avoid eggs, substitute 1 ½ cups applesauce in the batter.

1. Preheat oven to 350° F. Spritz the baking dish lightly with cooking spray and set aside.

2. In a mixing bowl, combine the wheat-free flour blend, cinnamon, baking soda, baking powder, and salt.

3. In another mixing bowl, add the sugar, oil, vanilla extract, and eggs.

4. Using an electric mixer set to medium speed, mix the wet ingredients until blended.

5. Pour the wet ingredients into the bowl with dry ingredients. Mix on medium speed until smooth. Set aside.

6. Peel the apples with a vegetable peeler. Chop into small pieces.

7. Transfer half of the batter into the baking dish. Evenly sprinkle apples on top. Pour the remaining batter over them.

8. Place in the oven and bake for about 45 minutes, or until a toothpick comes out clean when inserted.

CINNAMON COOKIES

Sugar and spice and everything nice—and no wheat! Crispy on the outside, chewy on this inside, these cookies made with almond flour are easy to make and fun to eat!

Prep Time: 10 minutes

Cook Time: 25 minutes

Makes 1 dozen cookies

Ingredients

2 cups almond flour

¼ teaspoon baking soda

1 ½ teaspoons ground cinnamon

¼ cup pure maple syrup

4 tablespoons butter,
    softened to room temperature

Topping

½ teaspoon cinnamon

2 teaspoons sugar

optional: almond slivers

Tools

large baking sheet

parchment paper

mixing bowl

spoon

small mixing bowl

spatula

cooling rack

Allergen Alert!

If you need to avoid dairy,
substitute coconut oil for butter.
The coconut oil will give the cookies
a similar, yet tropical flavor!

If you have a nut allergy, use a
wheat-free flour blend and
leave the almond slivers off.

1. Preheat oven to 275°F. Line a large baking sheet with parchment paper and set aside.

2. In a mixing bowl, combine the almond flour, baking soda, ground cinnamon, and maple syrup.

3. Add the butter and mix well. Use your hands if it gets difficult to stir.

4. Split the dough into 12 equal pieces. Roll each piece into a ball.

5. In a small mixing bowl, combine the cinnamon and sugar. Roll the dough balls around in the mixture to lightly coat.

6. Place the dough balls on the baking sheet. Flatten them with the palm of your hand to make a circle shape. Place almond slivers on top if desired.

7. Place in the oven for about 15 minutes. Using a spatula, flip the cookies. Bake an additional 10 minutes.

8. Remove from oven. Allow to cool for five minutes before placing on a cooling rack.

9. Serve warm or at room temperature. Store leftovers in an airtight container for up to one week.

GLOSSARY

assemble—to put all the parts of something together

blend—to mix together, sometimes using a blender

boil—to heat until large bubbles form on top of a liquid; the boiling point for water is 212°F (100°C)

consume—to eat or drink something

mash—to smash a soft food into a lumpy mixture

pit—the single central seed or stone of certain fruits

pulp—the soft juicy or fleshy part of a fruit or vegetable

simmer—to keep just below boiling when cooking or heating

whisk—stir a mixture rapidly until it's smooth

READ MORE

Clark, Pamela. *Allergy-free Cooking for Kids.* New York: Sterling Epicure, 2014.

Cook, Deanna. *Cooking Class: 57 Fun Recipies Kids Will Love to Make (and Eat!).* North Adams, MA: Storey Publishing, 2015.

McAneney, Caitie. *Peanut and Other Food Allergies.* Let's Talk About It. New York: PowerKids Press, 2015.

INTERNET SITES

Use FactHound to find Internet sites related to this book. All of the sites on FactHound have been researched by our staff.

Here's all you do:

Visit *www.facthound.com*

Type in this code: 9781491480571